Xmas 1989.

For the peaceful
moments. Enjoy!

love
Joan.

A Modern Book of
HOURS

For Bruegel the Elder
and Frederica the Younger

A Modern Book of
HOURS

Illustrated by
Cherry Denman

EDITED BY JUDY MARTIN

Bulfinch Press
Little, Brown and Company
BOSTON TORONTO LONDON

First U.S. edition

ISBN 0-8212-1751-8

Library of Congress Catalog Card Number 88-84120

Conceived and produced by Breslich & Foss
Golden House, 28-31 Great Pulteney Street
London W1R 3DD

Designed by Peartree Design Associates

Bulfinch Press is an imprint and trademark of
Little, Brown and Company (Inc.)

*Published simultaneously in Canada
by Little, Brown & Company (Canada) Limited*

PRINTED IN BELGIUM

Contents

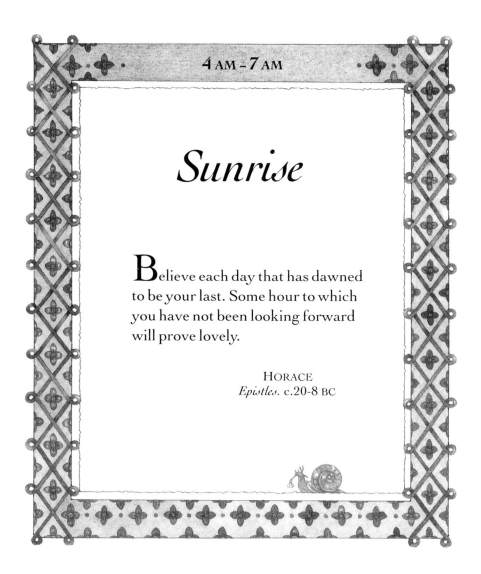

Sunrise

Believe each day that has dawned to be your last. Some hour to which you have not been looking forward will prove lovely.

HORACE
Epistles. c.20-8 BC

For what human ill does not dawn seem to be an alleviation?

THORNTON WILDER
The Bridge of San Luis Rey, 1927

The darkness of night, like pain, is dumb; the darkness of dawn, like peace, is silent.

RABINDRANATH TAGORE
Fireflies, 1928

...this is a piece too fair
To be the child of Chance and not of Care.
No Atoms casually together hurl'd
Could e'er produce so beautiful a world.

JOHN DRYDEN
To my Honoured Friend Sir Robert Howard
On His Excellent Poems, 1660

I am that which began;
   Out of me the years roll;
Out of me God and man;
   I am equal and whole;
God changes, and man, and the form of them bodily;
   I am the soul.

Before ever land was,
   Before ever the sea
Or soft hair of the grass,
   Or fair limbs of the tree,
Or the flesh-coloured fruit of the branches I was,
   And thy soul was in me.

A. C. SWINBURNE
Hertha

They were all night and dreaming; now it is day and they are vanished. They were spring flowers and, spring over, they are all faded together. They were a shadow, and it has travelled on beyond. They were smoke, and it has gone out in the air. They were bubbles and are broken. They were cobwebs and are swept away. And so this spiritual refrain is left again for us to sing; vanity of vanities, all is vanity.

JOHN CHRYSOSTOM
4th century AD

$\mathbf{T}$hou art a shadow and in love with the sun:
the sun comes, that shadow is naughted speedily.

JALÂL AL-DIN RÛMI
The Masnavi, 13th century

Don't be angry," said the Planet. "As you haven't been to the Hall of Heaven before and haven't yet been given a name, the Guardians don't know who you are and are quite right not to let you pass. When you have seen the Emperor and received your appointment, they will let you go in and out as you please." "That's as may be," said Monkey, "but at the present moment I can't get in."

WU CH'ENG-EN
Monkey (from *Hsi-yu chi*, 1592)
translation by Arthur Waley, 1942

Life can only
be understood
backwards; but it
must be lived forwards.

SOREN KIERKEGAARD
Stages on Life's Way, 1854

The One remains, the many change and pass;
Heaven's light remains, Earth's shadows fly;
Life, like a dome of many-coloured glass
Stains the white radiance of eternity,
Until Death tramples it to fragments.

PERCY BYSSHE SHELLEY
Adonais, 1821

RAPHAEL

The sun makes music as of old
 Amid the rival spheres of Heaven,
On its predestined circle rolled
 With thunder speed: the Angels even
Draw strength from gazing on its glance,
 Though none its meaning fathom may:
The world's unwithered countenance
 Is bright as on Creation's day.

GABRIEL

And swift and swift, with rapid lightness.
 The adornèd Earth spins silently,
Alternating Elysian brightness
 With deep and dreadful night; the sea
Foams in broad billows from the deep
 Up to the rocks, and rocks and ocean
Onward, with spheres which never sleep,
 Are hurried in eternal motion.

MICHAEL

And tempests in contention roar
   From land to sea, from sea to land;
And, raging, weave a chain of power,
   Which girds the earth, as with a band,
A flashing desolation there,
   Flames before the thunder's way;
But Thy servants, Lord, revere
   The gentle changes of Thy day.

CHORUS OF THE THREE

The Angels draw strength from Thy glance,
   Though no one comprehend Thee may:
The world's unwithered countenance
   Is bright as on Creation's day.

JOHANN WOLFGANG VON GOETHE
Faust, First Part, 1801

Some of the ancients, divining the truth
yet from far away, reckoned that
the soul knows things because
it is composed of them.

THOMAS AQUINAS
Philosophical Texts, 13th century

Or speak to the Earth, and it shall teach thee.

JOB 12.8

The earth does not argue,
Is not pathetic, has no arrangements,
Does not scream, haste, persuade,
  threaten, promise,
Makes no discriminations, has no
  conceivable failures,
Closes nothing, refuses nothing,
  shuts none out.

WALT WHITMAN
A Song of the Rolling Earth, 1860

May the Great Mystery make
sunrise in your heart.

SIOUX INDIAN SAYING

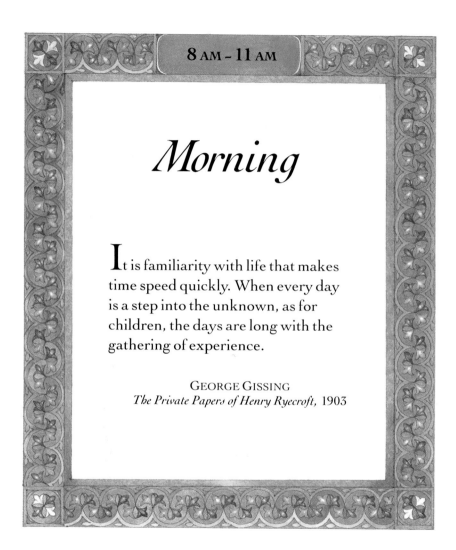

Morning

It is familiarity with life that makes time speed quickly. When every day is a step into the unknown, as for children, the days are long with the gathering of experience.

GEORGE GISSING
The Private Papers of Henry Ryecroft, 1903

Lose an hour in the morning and you will be all day hunting for it.

RICHARD WHATELY
Apophthegms, 1864

The boy who expects every morning to open into a new world finds that today is like yesterday, but he believes tomorrow will be different.

CHARLES DUDLEY WARNER
Backlog Studies, 1873

I don't know what I may seem to the world, but, as to myself, I seem to have been only like a boy playing on the sea shore, and diverting myself now and then finding a smoother pebble or a prettier shell than ordinary, whilst the great ocean of truth lay all undiscovered before me.

SIR ISAAC NEWTON
from *Brewster: Memoirs of Newton,* 1855

We should be careful to get out of an experience only the wisdom that is in it – and stay there, lest we be like the cat that sits down on a hot stove-lid. She will never sit down on a hot stove-lid again – and that is well; but also she will never sit down on a cold one anymore.

MARK TWAIN
Following the Equator, 1897

Life is painting a picture, not doing a sum.

OLIVER WENDELL HOLMES JR.
Speeches, 1913

Contact with children teaches us sincerity, simplicity, the habit of living in the present hour, the present action.

Children are, as it were, reborn daily: hence their spontaneity, the lack of complexity in their souls, the simplicity of their judgements and actions.

Moreover, their intuitive distinctions between good and evil are unencumbered, their souls are free of the bonds of sin, they are not under the necessity of weighing and analyzing.

We possess all this as a birthright which we wantonly scatter on our way, so that we must afterwards painfully gather up the fragments of our lost fortune.

FATHER ALEXANDER ELCHANINOV
Diary of a Russian Priest, publ. 1961

You never enjoy the world aright, till the sea itself gloweth in your veins, till you are clothed with the heavens and crowned with the stars; and perceive yourself to be the sole heir of the world, and more than so, because men are in it who are every one sole heirs as well as you.

THOMAS TRAHERNE
Centuries of Meditations, c.1665

The green lakes are sleeping in the mountain shadow, and on the water's canvas bright sunshine paints the picture of the day.

GWILYM COWLYD
from *A Celtic Miscellany*

I t is eternity now. I am in the midst of it. It is about me in the sunshine; I am in it, as the butterfly in the light-laden air. Nothing has to come; it is now. Now is eternity; now is the immortal life.

RICHARD JEFFERIES
The Story of My Heart, 1883

The same stream of life that runs through my veins night and day runs through the world and dances in rhythmic measures.

It is the same life that shoots in joy through the dust of the earth in numberless blades of grass and breaks into tumultuous waves of leaves and flowers.

It is the same life that is rocked in the ocean-cradle of birth and death, in ebb and in flow.

I feel my limbs are made glorious by the touch of this world of life. And my pride is from the life-throb of ages dancing in my blood this moment.

RABINDRANATH TAGORE
Gitanjali, 1910

W̲e are too little to be able always to rise above difficulties. Well, then, let us pass beneath them quite simply.

THÉRÈSE OF LISIEUX

I̲n nature there are neither rewards nor punishments – there are consequences.

ROBERT G. INGERSOLL
Some Reasons Why, 1896

The parallel between a whirlpool in a stream and a living being, which has often been drawn, is as just as it is striking. The whirlpool is permanent, but the particles of water which constitute it are incessantly changing. Those which enter it, on the one side, are whirled around and temporarily constitute a part of its individuality; and as they leave it on the other side, their places are made good by newcomers.

THOMAS HENRY HUXLEY
The Crayfish, 1888

To see the world in a Grain of Sand,
And a Heaven in a Wild Flower,
Hold Infinity in the palm of your hand
And Eternity in an hour.

WILLIAM BLAKE
Auguries of Innocence, c.1803

If the doors of perception were
cleansed, every thing would appear
to man as it is, infinite.

CHRISTOPHER SMART
A Song to David, 1763

The ways are two:
love and want of love.
That is all.

MENCIUS
Works, 3rd century BC

Noon

H e either fears his fate too much,
  Or his deserts are small,
That puts it not unto the touch
  To win or lose it all.

JAMES GRAHAM,
MARQUIS OF MONTROSE
My Dear and Only Love, 17th century

Live all you can; it's a mistake not to. It doesn't so much matter what you do in particular, so long as you have had your life. If you haven't had that, what have you had?

HENRY JAMES
The Ambassadors, 1903

They are ill discoverers that think there is no land when they can see nothing but sea.

FRANCIS BACON
Advancement of Learning, 1605

It is truly beyond human nature to possess wings and fly on high at one's own will. But to receive this gift of wings, almost contrary to nature, this is surely like the possession, strengthened by exercise, of a marvellous ability for contemplation, so that you may when you will, penetrate on the wing of clear sight into the difficult regions of secret knowledge.

RICHARD OF SAINT VICTOR
Benjamin Major, 12th century

That Light whose smile kindles the Universe,
That Beauty in which all things work and move,
That Benediction which the eclipsing Curse
Of birth can quench not, that sustaining Love
Which through the web of being blindly wove
By man and beast and earth and air and sea,
Burns bright or dim, as each are mirrors of
The fire for which all thirst; now beams on me,
Consuming the last clouds of cold mortality.

PERCY BYSSHE SHELLEY
Adonais, 1821

All seed-sowing is a mysterious thing, whether the seed fall into the earth or into souls. Man is a husbandman; his whole work rightly understood is to develop life, to sow it everywhere. Such is the mission of humanity, and of this divine mission the great instrument is speech. We too often forget that language is both a seed-sowing and a revelation.

HENRI FRÉDÈRIC AMIEL
Journal intime: entry for 2 May 1852

For that same sweet sin of lechery, I would say as the Friar said: "A young man and a young woman in a green arbour in a May morning – if God do not forgive it, I would."

SIR JOHN HARINGTON
Epigrams, 1615

To live is like to love – all reason is against it, and all healthy instinct for it.

SAMUEL BUTLER
Note-Books, 1912

Thus the sum of things is ever renewed, and mortal creatures live in mutual dependency on each other. Some nations wax strong, others diminish, and in a brief space all the races of living beings are changed. Like runners in a torch race, they hand forward the flame of life.

LUCRETIUS
De Rerum Natura, 1st century BC

The first thing to be said is that whatever religious faith, feelings and hopes we have, we are bound to shape them into form in life, not only at home, but in the work we do in the world. Whatever we feel justly we ought to shape; whatever we think, to give it clear form; whatever we have inside of us, our duty is to mould it outside of ourselves into clear speech or act, which, if it be loving, will be luminous.

STOPFORD BROOKE
*Religion in Literature and
Religion in Life,* 1900

There are days now and again when the summer broods in Trafalgar Square; the flood of light from a cloudless sky gathers and grows, thickening the air; the houses enclose the beams as water is enclosed in a cup . . . Either the light subdues the sound, or perhaps rather it renders the senses slumberous and less sensitive, but the great sunlit square is silent – silent, that is, for the largest city on earth. A slumberous silence of abundant light, of the full summer day, of the high flood of summer hours whose tide can rise no higher. A time to linger and dream under the beautiful breast of heaven, a heaven brooding and descending into pure light upon man's handiwork.

RICHARD JEFFERIES
The Life of the Fields, 1884

When that sun shines upon him the dust-bin of this world is changed for him into a rose garden; the kernel is seen beneath the rind.

FARÎD AL-DIN ÀTTÂR
13th century

With everything wrong right is somehow involved. Falsehood gets its glitter from truth. We seek base metal because we think it gold. Our delight in pursuing the bad comes from our belief that it is the good.

JALÂL-DIN RÛMI
The Masnavi, 13th century

It is more from carelessness about truth than from intentional lying, that there is so much falsehood in the world.

SAMUEL JOHNSON
Quoted in *Boswell's Life of Johnson*, dated 1776

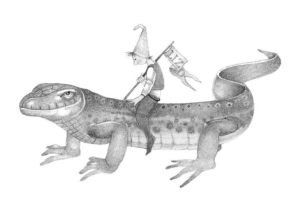

A lizard ran out on a rock and looked up,
listening no doubt to the sound of
the spheres.
And what a dandy fellow! the right toss of a chin
for you and swirl of a tail!

If men were as much men as lizards are lizards
they'd be worth looking at.

D. H. LAWRENCE
Lizard, 1929

All animals are living hieroglyphs,
The dashing dog, and stealthy-stepping cat,
Hawk, bull, and all that breathe mean something
   more
To the true eye than their shapes show; for all
Were made in love, and made to be beloved.
Thus must he think as to earth's lower life,
Who seeks to win the world to thought and love.

PHILIP J. BAILEY
Festus, 1839

It takes life to love life.

EDGAR LEE MASTERS
Spoon River Anthology, 1915

The bliss of the animals lies in this, that, on their lower level, they shadow the bliss of those – few at any moment on the earth – who do not "look before and after, and pine for what is not" but live in the holy carelessness of the eternal *now.*

GEORGE MACDONALD

Happiness is no laughing matter.

RICHARD WHATELY
Apophthegms, 1864

Afternoon

Experience is never limited and it is never complete; it is an immense sensibility, a kind of huge spider-web of the finest silken threads suspended in the chamber of consciousness, and catching every airborne particle in its tissue.

HENRY JAMES
Partial Portraits: The Art of Fiction, 1888

Desires are only the lack of something: and those who have the greatest desires are in a worse condition than those who have none, or very slight ones.

PLATO
Eryxias, 4th century BC

But all our best is of our own doing: such is our nature as long as we remain detached. The wise and the good do perform acts; their right action is the expression of their own power: in the others it comes in the breathing spaces when the passions are in abeyance; but it is not that they draw this occasional wisdom from outside themselves; simply, they are for the time being unhindered.

PLOTINUS
Treatises, c.253-270 AD

To regret one's own experiences is to arrest one's own development. To deny one's own experiences is to put a lie into the lips of one's own life. It is no less than a denial of the soul.

OSCAR WILDE
De Profundis, 1897

Men go abroad to wonder at the height of mountains, at the huge waves of the sea, at the long courses of the rivers, at the vast compasses of the ocean, at the circular motion of the stars, and they pass by themselves without wondering.

AUGUSTINE OF HIPPO
4th-5th century AD

Laughter is nothing else but sudden glory arising from some sudden conception of some eminency in ourselves, by comparison with the infirmity of others, or with our own formerly.

THOMAS HOBBES
Human Nature, 1650

I confess that I do not see why the very existence of an invisible world may not in part depend on the personal response which any one of us may make to the religious appeal. God himself, in short, may draw vital strength and increase from our very fidelity. For my own part, I do not know what the sweat and blood and tragedy of this life mean, if they mean anything short of this. If this life be not a real fight, in which something is eternally gained for the universe by success, it is no better than a private game of theatricals from which one may withdraw at will. But it feels like a real fight, – as if there were something wild in the universe

which we, with all our idealities and faithlessnesses, are needed to redeem: and first of all, to redeem our own hearts from our atheisms and fears. For such a half-wild half-saved universe is our nature adapted. The deepest thing in our nature is this dumb region of the heart in which we dwell alone with our willingnesses and unwillingnesses, our faiths and our fears . . .

These then are my last words to you: Be not afraid of life. Believe that life is worth living, and your belief will help create the fact.

WILLIAM JAMES
The Will to Believe, 1897

Conventionality is not morality. Self-righteousness is not religion. To attack the first is not to assail the last. To pluck the mask from the face of the Pharisee is not to lift an impious hand to the Crown of Thorns.

CHARLOTTE BRONTE
Preface to *Jane Eyre, 2nd edn,* 1847

The usual excuse of those who cause others trouble is that they wish them well.

MARQUIS DE VAUVENARGUES
Reflections and Maxims, 1746

Better trust all and be deceived,
　And weep that trust and that deceiving,
Than doubt one heart that, if believed,
　Had blessed one's life with true believing.

FANNY KEMBLE

I made my song a coat
Covered with embroideries
Out of old mythologies
From heel to throat;
But the fools caught it,
Wore it in the world's eyes
As though they'd wrought it.
Song, let them take it,
For there's more enterprise
In walking naked.

W. B. YEATS
A Coat, 1913

It is impossible for a man to be made happy by putting him in a happy place, unless he be first in a happy state.

BENJAMIN WHICHCOTE
Moral and Religious Aphorisms, 1753

As the bee collects nectar and departs without injuring the flower, or its colour or scent, so let a sage dwell in his village.

DHAMMAPADA
3rd century BC

Words are not crystal, transparent and unchanged; they are the skin of living thoughts and may vary greatly in colour and content according to the circumstances and time in which they are used.

OLIVER WENDELL HOLMES

I am not eternity but a man; a part of the whole, as an hour is of the day.

EPICTETUS
Discourses 2.5, 2nd century AD

To a great experience, one thing is essential, an experiencing nature.

WALTER BAGEHOT
Literary Studies, 1879

Dusk

Lost, yesterday, somewhere between Sunrise and Sunset, two golden hours, each set with sixty diamond minutes. No reward is offered, for they are gone forever.

HORACE MANN
Lost, Two Golden Hours

When the sun sets, shadows, that showed at noon but small, appear most long and terrible

NATHANIEL LEE
Oedipus, 1697

What is true in the lamplight is not always true in the sunlight.

JOSEPH JOUBERT
Pensées, 1842

There rolls the deep where grew the tree,
   O Earth, what changes thou has seen!
   There where the long street roars hath been
The stillness of the central sea.

The hills are shadows, and they flow
   From form to form, and nothing stands;
   They melt like mist, the solid lands,
Like clouds they shape themselves and go.

ALFRED, LORD TENNYSON
In Memoriam A.H.H., 1833-50

Into my heart an air that kills
   From yon far country blows:
What are those blue remembered hills,
   What spires, what farms are those?

That is the land of lost content,
   I see it shining plain,
The happy highways where I went
   And cannot come again.

A. E. HOUSEMAN
A Shropshire Lad, 1896

Sometimes I felt very lonely, depressed and ill. I'd often repeat to myself a line of poetry which brought peace and strength back into my soul; it runs, "Time's but a ship that bears thee, not thy home." That image appeals to me and helps me to bear the exile of this life.

THÉRÈSE OF LISIEUX
The Story of a Little White Flower, 1895-96

There must be either a predestined Necessity and inviolable plan, or a gracious Providence, or chaos without design or director. If then there be an inevitable Necessity, why kick against the pricks? If a Providence that is ready to be gracious, render thyself worthy of a divine succour. But if a chaos without guide, congratulate thyself that amid such a surging sea thou hast in thyself a guiding Reason.

MARCUS AURELIUS
Meditations, 2nd century AD

He who regards the world as he does the fortunes of his own body can govern the world. He who loves the world as he does his own body can be entrusted with the world.

LAO TSU
Tao Te Ching, 6th century BC

Enquire of the man who hath gotten himself wealth, if he hath also assured himself of the years of his life.

JOSEPH KIMCHI OF NARBONNE
Shekel Hakodesh, 12th century

When you have nothing to say, say nothing.

CHARLES CALEB COLTON
Lacon, 1820

The scenes of our lives are like pictures done in rough mosaic. Looked at close, they produce no effect. There is nothing beautiful to be found in them, unless you stand some distance off.

ARTHUR SCHOPENHAUER
Parerga and Paralipomena, 1851

The spirit of wisdom cannot be delineated with pen and ink, no more than a sound can be painted, or the wind grasped in the hollow of the hand.

JOHN SPARROW
Preface to *Boehme's Signatura Rerum,* 17th century

Slender at first, they quickly gather force,
Growing in richness as they run their course;
Once started, they do not turn back again:
Rivers, and years, and friendships with good men.

SANSKRIT POEM

We are the music makers,
 We are the dreamers of dreams,
Wandering by lone sea breakers,
 And sitting by desolate streams;-
World-losers and world-forsakers,
 On whom the pale moon gleams:
We are the movers and shakers
 Of the world forever, it seems.

ARTHUR O'SHAUGHNESSY
Ode

Man prays for evil as he prays
for good: for man was ever hasty.

KORAN XVII.11

By doubting we are led to enquire;
by enquiry we perceive the truth.

PIERRE ABELARD
12th century

He who doubts from what he sees
Will ne'er believe, do what you please.
If the Sun and Moon should doubt,
They'd immediately go out.

WILLIAM BLAKE
Auguries of Innocence, c.1803

One can live in the shadow of an idea without grasping it.

ELIZABETH BOWEN
The Heat of the Day, 1949

Wear your worries like a loose garment.

ANON

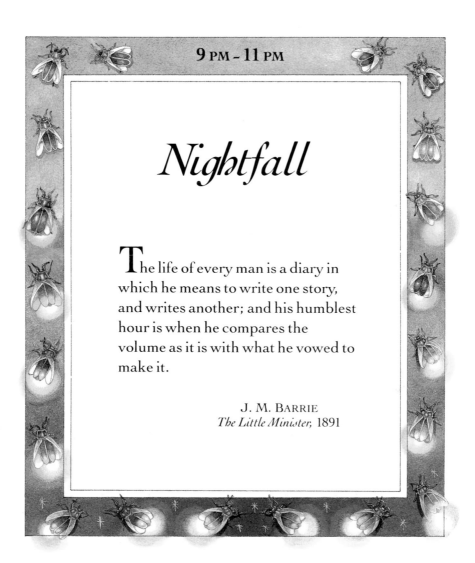

Nightfall

The life of every man is a diary in which he means to write one story, and writes another; and his humblest hour is when he compares the volume as it is with what he vowed to make it.

J. M. BARRIE
The Little Minister, 1891

I remember my youth and the feeling that will never come back any more – the feeling that I could last forever, outlast the sea, the earth and all men; the deceitful feeling that lures us on to perils, to love, to vain effort – to death; the triumphant conviction of strength, the heat of life in the handful of dust, that glow in the heart that with every year grows dim, grows cold, grows small, and expires – and expires, too soon, too soon, before life itself.

JOSEPH CONRAD
Youth, 1898

Good men are bad men's instructors,
And bad men are good men's materials.

LAO TSE
Tao Te Ching, 6th century BC

But, when the days of golden dreams had perished,
And even Despair was powerless to destroy,
Then did I learn how existence could be cherished,
Strengthened, and fed without the aid of joy.

EMILY BRONTE
Remembrance, 1846

There is, brethren, a condition wherein there is neither earth, nor water, nor fire, nor air, nor the sphere of infinite space, nor the sphere of infinite consciousness, nor the sphere of the void, nor the sphere of either perception or non-perception: where there is no "this world" and no "world beyond": where there is no moon and no sun. That condition, brethren, do I call neither a coming nor a going nor a standing still nor a falling away nor a rising up: but it is without fixity, without mobility, without basis. That is the end of woe.

UDANA

Who know the world live alone.

ÀLÎ IBN ABÛ TÂLIB
7th century

If all mankind were of one opinion, and only one person were of the contrary opinion, mankind would be no more justified in silencing that one person than he, if he had the power, would be justified in silencing mankind.

JOHN STUART MILL
On Liberty, 1859

The universe is, I conceive, like to a great game being played out, and we poor mortals are allowed to take a hand. By great good fortune, the wiser among us have made out some few rules of the game, as at present played. We call them "Laws of Nature", and honour them because we find that if we obey them we win something for our pains. The cards are our theories and hypotheses, the tricks our experimental verifications.

THOMAS HENRY HUXLEY
from *Life and Letters*, 1900

What is now proved was once only imagined.

WILLIAM BLAKE
The Marriage of Heaven and Hell, 1790-93

Life does not cease to be funny when people die, any more than it ceases to be serious when people laugh.

GEORGE BERNARD SHAW
The Doctor's Dilemma, 1913

There is in us something wiser than our head.

ARTHUR SCHOPENHAUER
Parerga and Paralipomena, 1851

The years teach us much which the days never knew.

RALPH WALDO EMERSON
Essays, 1844

When you are old and grey and full of sleep,
And nodding by the fire, take down this book,
And slowly read, and dream of the soft look
Your eyes once had, and of their shadows deep.

How many loved your moments of glad grace,
And loved your beauty with love false or true,
But one man loved the pilgrim soul in you,
And loved the sorrows of your changing face;

And bending down beside the glowing bars,
Murmur, a little sadly, how Love fled
And paced upon the mountains overhead
And hid his face amid a crown of stars.

W. B. YEATS
When You Are Old, 1893

Men fear death as children fear to go into the
dark; and as that natural fear in children is
increased with tales, so is the other.

FRANCIS BACON
Essays, 1625

W e are all in the gutter, but some
of us are looking at the stars.

OSCAR WILDE
Lady Windermere's Fan, 1892

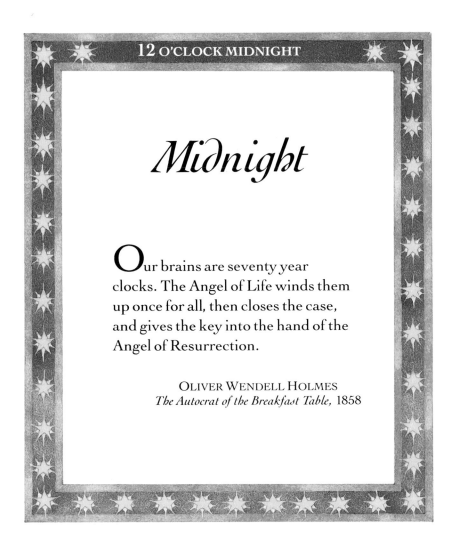

Midnight

Our brains are seventy year clocks. The Angel of Life winds them up once for all, then closes the case, and gives the key into the hand of the Angel of Resurrection.

OLIVER WENDELL HOLMES
The Autocrat of the Breakfast Table, 1858

Both in thought and in feeling, even though time be real, to realize the unimportance of time is the gate of wisdom.

BERTRAND RUSSELL
Mysticism and Logic, 1917

I worry until midnight, and from then on I let God worry.

BLESSED LOUIS GUANELLA

There is something haunting in the light of the moon; it has all the dispassionateness of a disembodied soul, and something of its inconceivable mystery.

JOSEPH CONRAD
Lord Jim, 1900

The pieces move, now few, now more;
Here many, where before was one,
Here none, where many stood before.
Time, with the goddess Death at play,
Sits at the chequer-board and rolls
Alternate dice of night and day,
And takes the pieces, living souls
Of all that dwell beneath the sun.

SANSKRIT POEM
5th-6th century BC

One must take all one's life to learn how to live, and, what will perhaps make you wonder more, one must take all one's life to learn how to die.

SENECA
On the Shortness of Life, 1st century AD

Science says: 'We must live', and seeks the means of prolonging, increasing, facilitating and amplifying life, of making it tolerable and acceptable; wisdom says: 'We must die', and seeks how to make us die well.

MIGUEL DE UNAMO
Essays and Soliloquies, 1924

His helmet now shall make an hive for bees,
And lovers' sonnets turn'd to holy psalms:
A man at arms must now serve on his knees,
And feed on prayers, that are old age's alms:

GEORGE PEELE
Sonnet Ad Finem: A Farewell To Arms, 1590

The young have aspirations that never come to pass; the old have reminiscences of what never happened.

SAKI (H. H. MUNRO)

There is a certain relief in change, even though it be from bad to worse, as I have found in travelling in a stage-coach, that it is often a comfort to shift one's position and be bruised in a new place.

WASHINGTON IRVING
Tales of a Traveller, 1824

Time ought, above all other kinds of property, to be free from invasion, and yet there is no man who does not claim the power of wasting that time which is the right of others.

SAMUEL JOHNSON
The Idler, 1758

Does the road wind up-hill all the way?
 Yes, to the very end.
Will the day's journey take the whole long day?
 From morn to night, my friend.

But is there for the night a resting-place?
 A roof for when the slow dark hours begin.
May not the darkness hide it from my face?
 You cannot miss that inn.

Shall I meet other wayfarers at night?
 Those who have gone before.
Then must I knock, or call when just in sight?
 They will not keep you standing at that door.

Shall I find comfort, travel-sore and weak?
 Of labour you shall find the sum.
Will there be beds for me and all who seek?
 Yea, beds for all who come.

CHRISTINA ROSSETTI
Up-hill, 1858

Out of the night that covers me,
  Black as the pit from pole to pole,
I thank whatever gods may be
  For my unconquerable soul.

W. E. HENLEY
Invictus, 1888

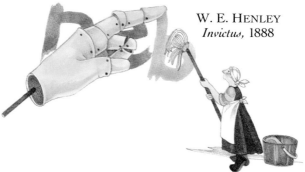

The Moving Finger writes, and having writ
Moves on: nor all your Piety nor Wit,
Shall lure it back to cancel half a Line,
Nor all your Tears wash out a Word of it.

EDWARD FITZGERALD
The Rubáiyat of Omar Khayyam, 1859

Down, down, down into the darkness of
the grave
Gently they go, the beautiful, the tender,
the kind;
Quietly they go, the intelligent, the witty,
the brave.
I know. But I do not approve. And I am
not resigned.

EDNA ST VINCENT MILLAY
Dirge without Music, 1928

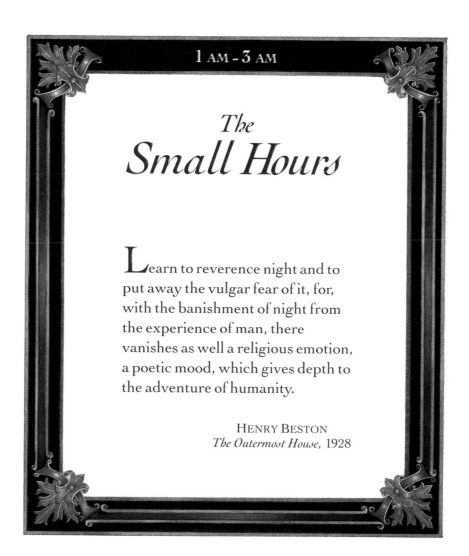

The
Small Hours

Learn to reverence night and to put away the vulgar fear of it, for, with the banishment of night from the experience of man, there vanishes as well a religious emotion, a poetic mood, which gives depth to the adventure of humanity.

HENRY BESTON
The Outermost House, 1928

I dimly guess what Time in mists confounds;
Yet ever and anon a trumpet sounds
From the hid battlements of Eternity.

FRANCIS THOMPSON
The Hound of Heaven, 1890-92

W e love life, not because we are used to living,
but because we are used to loving.

FRIEDRICH NIETZSCHE
Thus Spoke Zarathustra, 1883-92

To write so as to bring home to the heart, the heart must have been tried, – but, perhaps, ceased to be so. While you are under the influence of passions, you only feel, but cannot describe them, – any more than, when in action, you could turn round and tell the story to your next neighbour. When all is over, – all, all and irrevocable, – trust to memory – she is then but too faithful . . .

GEORGE GORDON, LORD BYRON
Journal, 20th February 1814

Pity is the feeling which arrests the mind in the presence of whatsoever is grave and constant in human sufferings and unites it with the human sufferer. Terror is the feeling which arrests the mind in the presence of whatsoever is grave and constant in human sufferings and unites it with the secret cause.

JAMES JOYCE
A Portrait of the Artist as a Young Man, 1916

In Sleep we lie all naked and alone, in Sleep we are united at the heart of night and darkness, and we are strange and beautiful asleep; for we are dying in the darkness, and we know no death.

THOMAS WOLFE
From Death to Morning, 1935

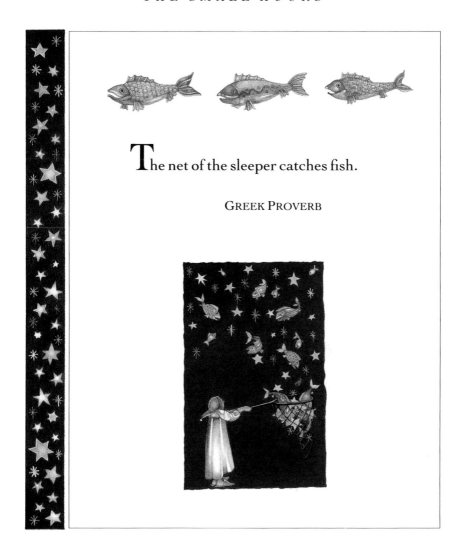

The net of the sleeper catches fish.

GREEK PROVERB

I strove with none, for none was worth my
   strife;
Nature I loved, and next to nature, art;
I warmed both hands before the fire of life;
It sinks, and I am ready to depart.

                    WALTER SAVAGE LANDOR
                       Finis, 1853

My soul, sit thou a patient looker-on,
  Judge not the play until the play is done,
Her plot hath many changes; every day
Speaks a new scene; the last act crowns the play.

FRANCIS QUARLES
Respice Finem

Be cheerful, sir.
Our revels now are ended. These our actors,
As I foretold you, were all spirits, and
Are melted into air, into thin air;
And, like the baseless fabric of this vision,
The cloud-capped towers, the gorgeous palaces,
The solemn temples, the great globe itself,
Yea, all which it inherit, shall dissolve,
And, like this insubstantial pageant faded,
Leave not a rack behind. We are such stuff
As dreams are made on; and our little life
Is rounded with a sleep.

WILLIAM SHAKESPEARE
The Tempest, 1611

He is the happiest man who can trace an unbroken connection between the end of his life and the beginning.

JOHANN WOLFGANG VON GOETHE
Maxims and Reflections

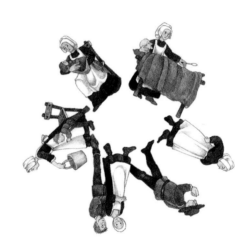

There is little difference between what one calls a long life and a short one. After all, it is but a moment in the indefinity of time.

Once upon a time I dreamed I was a butterfly, fluttering hither and thither, to all intents and purposes a butterfly. I was conscious only of following my fancies as a butterfly, and was unconscious of my individuality as a man. Suddenly I woke, and there I lay, myself again. Now I do not know whether I was then a man dreaming I was a butterfly, or whether I am now a butterfly dreaming I am a man.

CHUANG-TSE
3rd century BC

Time goes, you say? Ah no!
Alas, Time stays, *we* go.

HENRY AUSTIN DOBSON
The Paradox of Time, 1875

ACKNOWLEDGMENTS

8 Reprinted by permission of Macmillan Publishing Company, London and New York, from *Fireflies* by Rabindranath Tagore. © 1928 by Rabindranath Tagore, copyright renewed 1955
13 From *Monkey* by Wu Ch'eng-en, translated by Arthur Waley. Reprinted by permisson of Unwin Hyman Ltd, London and Harper & Row Publishers, Inc., New York
25 Reprinted by permission of Faber & Faber from *Diary of a Russian Priest*, by Alexander Elchaninov
27 From *A Celtic Miscellany* by K. Hurlstone Jackson. Reproduced by permission of Routledge & Kegan Paul Ltd
60, 89 'A Coat' and 'When You Are Old' from *The Collected Poems* by W. B. Yeats. Reprinted by permission of A.P. Watt Ltd on behalf of Michael B. Yeats and Macmillan London Ltd.
74, 96 From *Poems from the Sanskrit*, translated by John Brough (Penguin Classics, 1968) © John Brough 1968. Reproduced by permission of Penguin Books Ltd
77 From *The Heat of the Day* by Elizabeth Bowen, reproduced by permission of Curtis Brown Ltd, London, and Jonathan Cape on behalf of the author's estate; and by permission of Alfred A. Knopf, Inc., New York

87 From *The Doctor's Dilemma* by George Bernard Shaw. Reprinted by permission of The Society of Authors on behalf of the Bernard Shaw Estate
94 From *Mysticism and Logic* by Bertrand Russell, reprinted by permission of Unwin Hyman Ltd
105 Excerpt from 'Dirge without Music' by Edna St. Vincent Millay. From *Collected Poems*, Harper & Row. Copyright © 1928, 1955 by Edna St. Vincent Millay and Norma Millay Ellis. Reprinted by permission.
111 From *A Portrait of the Artist as a Young Man* by James Joyce. Reprinted by permission of The Society of Authors as literary representative of the Estate of James Joyce.

Every effort has been made to check attributions and obtain permission from copyright holders. The editor apologizes for any errors or omissions which may have occurred.

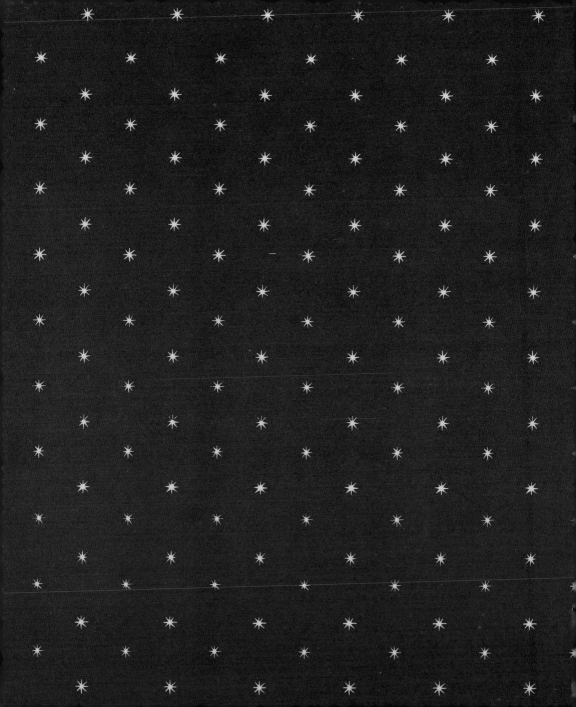